IT ONLY TAKES
EVERYTHING
YOU'VE GOT!

LESSONS FOR A LIFE OF SUCCESS

JULIO MELARA

It Only Takes Everything You've Got!

By

Julio A. Melara
1-800-355-TIME

It Only Takes Everything You've Got!
ISBN 0-9642430-1-6

Cover Design by James Ware
Printed in the U.S.A by Triumphant Publishers International

To order this title by mail, please include price as noted above, $2.50 handling per order, and $1.00 for each book ordered. Send to: Time for Action, 5757 Corporate Boulevard, Suite 402, Baton Rouge, Louisiana 70808.

Or call toll-free 1-800-355-TIME to order using VISA or Mastercard, or for further information on Julio A. Melara.

To Live Your Dreams You Must Wake Up!

(Most people over sleep)

It Only Takes Everything You've Got!

TABLE OF CONTENTS

DEDICATION

I dedicate this book to every person who is facing obstacles in the pursuit of their dream. Life is full of obstacles. Whether it's starting a business, buying a house, raising a family, going to college, making a sale, getting promoted, making more money or making something happen. It is not easy, but once your mind is focused and you take action, all things are possible.

IT ONLY TAKES EVERYTHING YOU'VE GOT!

- Julio A. Melara

ACKNOWLEDGEMENTS

A special thanks to the people who contributed to this project. To my wonderful wife and constant partner, Sherry. To Rolfe H. McCollister, Jr., for your friendship and constant encouragement. To Jeffrey Gitomer, for your unspeakably creative support and criticism. To Karen Rowley, DeAnna Brewer, Suzy Montalbano, Laura Ketteringham, Chris Holton, Becky Vance, Jennifer Ovington and James Ware, for all of your invaluable assistance in the development of this book. Gracias!

It Only Takes Everything You've Got!

FOREWORD

What Does it take to become a Success?
Every morning I get up and do three things -- read,
write and run. I've been reading for twenty-five
years. I've been writing for seven years, and I've
been running for three years.

Reading gets my attitude right for the day.
Writing gets my creativity juices flowing. And
running gets my body in better shape. Running
does not help you live longer, it just seems longer.
To get the running into perspective with the rest
of my self-disciplines I ordered a dozen T-shirts from
Julio Melara that say, "It Only Takes Everything
You've Got." I put one on every morning before
I run. Just having the shirt on reminds me of
what it takes to be the best.

Julio Melara is on a quest to be the best. When
I first saw him give a presentation I knew he had the
talent and the gift. He also had the self confidence.
Since that day we have become friends -- not by
actions alone-- but by the forces of God. We were
meant to be friends. It just took a few years to
meet. The two best parts about Julio is that he is
a student every day, and he has an internal flame
that is always lit. When you get to know him

you'll start to put the word "baby" at the end of every-thing. It's a Julio-word that adds his enthusiastic touch to everything he says. Julio is on fire.

This book will reveal his secret of the attitude and passion it takes to accomplish things. Today. But I challenge you to read the book, and read between the lines of the book. The words will give you the message -- what's in between the lines will give you the fire to make the message transferable to you. But be careful. If you decide to go for it -- It only takes everything you've got!

Jeffrey Gitomer,
Author of The Sales Bible

It Only Takes Everything You've Got!

It Only Takes

Everything

You've Got!

(Nothing More)

MENTAL APPETIZER

Truth will always be truth,
regardless of disbelief,
lack of understanding,
or ignorance.

W. Clement Stone

LESSON 1

YOU GOTTA WANNA

It was a Thursday afternoon and I had just finished giving a speech at the University of New Orleans. I was signing copies of my first book at the back table when a gentleman in his mid-50s came up to me. He asked me to write something special in the book for his 22-year-old son who was having all sorts of problems at this stage of his life. I agreed to write a special note and returned the book to him. About 25 minutes later, the gentleman returned to the table and got right in my face. He said, "Mr. Melara you gave me something today, now let me give something to you."

He continued, " When I was 13 years old, I ran away from home, quit school, did drugs and hung around with the wrong crowd." By the time he was 28, he said, he was tired of being a bum so he decided to pursue a GED. He received his GED, enrolled in college and after the first week of school became discouraged. He went to his professor and explained his discouragement, told him how he didn't have any family support, that he was working more than 50 hours a week to pay for his tuition, and that it was tough riding the public transit system back and forth.

After listening to 15 minutes of complaining, the professor looked at the young man and said, "Enough--forget about the past, where you have been and what you have done. I have one simple question for you today. He asked, "Are you willing to pay the price for success?" Because if you are not willing to pay the price for success, you will pay the price for failure.

All of a sudden, the man's eyes grew larger as he shared his story and right before he walked away, he gave me his business card. As I looked at his card, I read with amazement that he was now a special projects engineer with NASA. As chills went through my body, I thought deeply for the next few minutes about how right he was. One way or another there is a price to pay in life. The question is not, are we going to pay a price, but what price are we going to pay? A fact of life is that there is a price to pay, to be successful in business, to have a good marriage, to prosper spiritually, intellectually, emotionally, and physically. The question is, "Are you willing to pay this price?"

NOW IS THE TIME TO PAY

We live in incredible times on planet Earth. There is so much stress, pressure, uncertainty, and worry in our world today. People are concerned about the changes taking place in technology, the global economy, our youth, government, and everything else for that matter. Many people don't realize that change is part of life, and that the only thing constant in life is change. We are not in control of our lives, but the principles that God has put in motion are. Unless we understand what those principles are, understand how they function, and put them into action, we will never be fulfilled.

I am amazed at the thousands of people I meet every year who want to change their circumstances, but don't want to change themselves. People who want more money, but refuse to work harder. People who want success, but are not willing to pay the price. In order to change your external circumstances, you must change the things going on inside your minds and hearts. You must re-examine and re-evaluate the way you think and the way you respond to life's daily challenges. It all begins with taking action. You gotta wanna.

NOTHING BUT THE TRUTH

So many times I am introduced as a motivational speaker and I always make a point to explain that I am not a motivational speaker, but a motivated speaker. Why? Because I believe that only one thing motivates -- THE TRUTH. I can get you excited for an hour and maybe even for a day, but true motivation comes from within. When people find out the truth about what they can become and what they can achieve, it changes the course of their lives.

This book is about the truth. The first major premise of this book is that success is not dependent upon having superior intelligence, special skills, formal education, the ability to work hard, or luck. The world is full of highly educated and skilled people who experience ongoing frustration because of their lack of success. Thousands of people are working hard only to die impoverished and unfulfilled. What people need is a clear understanding and strategy for viewing their potential and mapping out their goals, goals that are truly worthwhile, believable, and achievable.

The second premise is that your life only becomes better when you become better. The difference between successful and unsuccessful people isn't nearly as great as most people believe. In fact, the difference is really slim. Successful people learn to develop simple strategies and skills that enable them to grow and create opportunities from challenges. We will explore this in more detail later.

And finally, the last major premise of this book is that success is a matter of understanding and putting into action the lessons, truths, habits, principles, and disciplines that have been around since the beginning of mankind. While this may not be a great revelation, you need to remember that they work, can be learned, and applied by anyone who is willing to put forth the necessary effort.

Proverbs 23:23 says, "Buy the truth and do not sell it; get wisdom, discipline and understanding." The truths, lessons, and principles discussed in this book are relatively simple but not easy, and none of them will work unless you do. You gotta wanna.

IT ONLY TAKES EVERYTHING YOU'VE GOT!

MENTAL DESSERT

*You and I do not see
things as they are.
We see things as we are.*

Herb Cohen

MENTAL APPETIZER

Live to learn and you will learn to live.

Author Unknown

LESSON **2**

LIFE IS A UNIVERSITY

A wise man once said that God gave man two ends-- one to sit on and one to think with. It has been evident ever since that the success or failure of any individual was dependent on the one he used most. Unfortunately, too many people today are sitting on their rear ends, not realizing that the way they think causes their problems. They have to straighten out the way they think if they are to improve their quality of life and achieve all of their dreams.

How do you straighten out the way you think? First, you must realize that life is a university. The university has an infinite number of lessons and curricula that are mandatory. Of course, you can choose to skip certain classes and never reach your full potential and achieve all you were meant to. If you try to cheat on tests or copy other people's homework, you are guaranteed an F. But if you choose to go to class every day, take notes, study, and put the principles into action, you will receive and achieve all you have ever dreamed.

Let me put it another way. Unless you learn and become aware of your purpose in life and

God's principles operating in the universe, you will never become fulfilled. Many years ago I began to study the traits and biographies of some of the most successful people in our country. Even today, I am constantly reading and searching for information that can help me grow in every area of my life.

One recent study I came across was by the sociologist, Dr. Anthony Campolo. He told about a sociological study of 50 people over the age of 95 who were asked, "If you could live your life over again, what would you do differently?" It was an open-ended question, and an array of answers came from these senior citizens. However, three answers dominated. They were:

• If I had it to do over again, I would reflect more.

• If I had it to do over again, I would risk more.

• If I had it to do over again, I would do more things that would live on after I am dead.

The time to learn to live is now, not tomorrow, and not when you get to be 95 ... if you make it that far. Today is the day for action. Why? Because if you live to learn, then you will learn to live. You will enjoy a life of purpose and meaning.

There is a funny scene about the purpose and meaning of life in the movie "City Slickers". Billy Crystal and two cohorts are about to hit 40. They are discussing and searching for the meaning of life. In one scene, here is what Billy says to a classroom full of young people:

"Value this time in your life, kids. This is the time when you still have your choices.

It goes by so fast.

When you are a teenager, you think you can do anything and -- you do.

Your 20s are a blur.

30s raise your family. You make a little money. You say to yourself- - 'What happened to my 20s?'

40s grow a little pot belly; grow another chin. Music starts to get too loud. One of your old girlfriends from high school becomes a grandmother.

50s you have minor surgery-- you call it a procedure-- but it's a surgery.

60s you have a major surgery. The music is still too loud, but it doesn't matter because you can't hear it anyway.

70s you and the wife retire to Fort Lauderdale. You start eating your dinner at 2 o'clock in the afternoon. You have lunch at 10 and breakfast the night before. Spend most of your time wandering the mall looking for the ultimate soft yogurt and muttering 'How come the kids don't call, how come the kids don't call?'

The 80s you will have a major stroke. You end up babbling to a Jamaican nurse your wife can't stand, but you call Momma. Any questions?"

Unfortunately many people either consciously or unconsciously look at life this way. The days just pass by. While some days and weeks are long, the years go by quickly with age.

Don't be fooled. Just having the means to live is not enough; a person must have something to live for. Your life must have meaning. True success means fulfillment. After all, when you get right down to it, everyone wants to enjoy success in every area of their lives. From family and career to finances and spiritual lives, everyone desires to prosper and be fulfilled.

After you realize and understand that life is a university and that knowledge is the passport to success, then that knowledge has to be put into action.

Nothing ever happens unless you put what you learn and know into action. There is a wise old saying I am sure you have heard-- "Give a man a fish and feed him for a day. But teach a man to fish and feed him for life." That is the spirit behind this book.

IT ONLY TAKES EVERYTHING YOU'VE GOT!

MENTAL DESSERT

*Few things are impossible
to diligence and skill...
great works are
performed not by
strength, but perseverance.*

Samuel Johnson

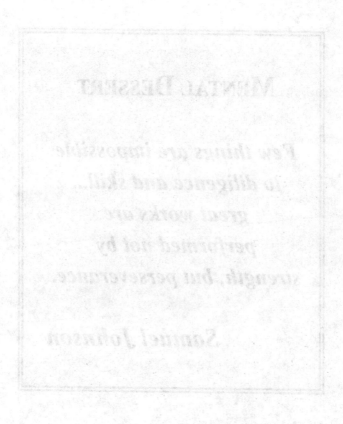

MENTAL APPETIZER

Any fact facing us is not as important as our attitude toward it, for that determines our success or failure.

Norman Vincent Peale

LESSON **3**

WE NEED P.R. BAD!
(Personal Responsibility)

One of the greatest problems facing America today is the lack of P.R. (Personal Responsibility). Many people want to blame the government, their spouses, children, family, economy, clients, and anyone else for their situation, but not themselves. While you and I cannot control our gender, the color of our skin, who our parents are, or where we grew up, there is one thing we can control -- Our Attitude!

If you are to achieve and live your dreams, you must take 100 percent responsibility for your life. It's been said that our potential is God's gift to us, and what we do with it is our gift to Him. It all starts with your attitude.

Your attitude, not your education, intelligence, contacts, or even hard work, is the main factor that determines whether you will accomplish your goals and live your dream. Attitude determines how far you can go on the success journey. A Fortune 500 study found that 94 percent of all executives surveyed attributed their success more to attitude than any other factor.[1]

The great psychologist-philosopher William James said, "The greatest discovery of my generation is that people can alter their lives by altering their attitudes of mind." He was right. The choices you have made up to now are the result of your attitude.

IT IS ABOUT ATTITUDE

All throughout high school and college, I struggled in English courses. When I was 26 years old, I began to think about the possibility of writing a book one day. Over the coming months, I decided that if a book were going to be written, I would have to start it and finish it, so I did. The process took more than two years, little by little, and I can still remember some friends and family questioning my ability to write a book.

However, I had the right attitude. I was determined to write my first book. Two years later I was finished, but there was a problem. Who was going to publish the book? I began to explore different venues and sent letters out to book publishers. Most did not respond, and one sent back a letter of rejection. Even though it was discouraging at times, I was determined and had the attitude that nothing was going to stop me. So I decided to self-publish the book, and on Aug. 3, 1994, my dream came true.

My first book, entitled "Do You Have Time for Success?", was published. The following year, a publishing company picked it up, and two-and-a-half years later, I received my first royalty check. But more importantly, the book was on its way to printing 75,000 copies and being sold nationwide. Why did it all happen? My Attitude!

Realize that your attitude determines your actions and actions determine your achievements. The person you are is the result of your attitude and choices.

One of the greatest men I admire and whose biography has impacted me is Abraham Lincoln. You will see examples of why throughout this book. One classic story I read about Abraham Lincoln showed clearly the relationship between our choices and their effect on who we are. An adviser to President Lincoln recommended a particular person for a Cabinet position, but Lincoln balked at the suggestion. He said, "I don't like the man's face." "But sir," said the adviser, "He can't be held responsible for his face." Lincoln replied, "Every man over 40 is responsible for his face." Who you are and how you think can be read in your face, too!

BACK TO PERSONAL RESPONSIBILITY

No one likes to do business with, or be friends with, people who have bad attitudes. People with bad attitudes cannot blame their attitude on anything or anyone but themselves. Forget about the past today. Yesterday is history. No one but you is responsible for the choices you make today. No matter what upbringing, bad circumstance, or obstacles you've had, you can change. No matter how negative your attitudes have been in the past, you can be more positive today. It begins with making a commitment to transform your mind daily by feeding it positive and motivational food. By becoming good stewards of your minds and programming them with the right knowledge and information, you maintain the right attitude in every situation. It is not easy, but it is definitely worth it. Having a positive attitude worked for me, and it will work for you!

POSITIVE ATTITUDE

A positive attitude is not just a feeling, it is a state of mind and a commitment. Your thoughts plus feelings equal your attitude. Having a positive attitude will not only affect your ability to succeed in business, but will also touch every aspect of your life, including your health. It is a fact that you can go a lot further in life and live longer with a positive attitude than you can without one.

Here is what a few great men have said about attitude:

"Things turn out the best for the people who make the best of the way things turn out."
John Wooden

"Nothing can stop the man with the right attitude from achieving his goal; nothing on earth can help the man with the wrong mental attitude."
W.W. Zeige

"Ability is what you are capable of doing. Motivation determines what you do, Attitude determines how well you do it."
Lou Holtz

"The last of the human freedoms is to choose one's attitude in any given set of circumstances."
Victor Frankel

"Attitude more than age determines energy."
Robert Schuller

"It is our attitude at the beginning of a difficult undertaking which, more than anything else, will determine its successful outcome."

William James

A positive attitude is more than seeing the glass half-full instead of half-empty. It is about being solution-oriented, not problem-oriented, belief not unbelief. It is about loving people and seeing the good in them. It is the ability to see opportunity in every obstacle that comes. It is about being persistent and determined, not discouraged and depressed.

A positive attitude is the willingness to take responsibility for your own life. You must be willing to step up and take full responsibility for your thoughts, choices, and actions. Only when you have taken full responsibility for yourself can you begin to change and move forward. The quality of your life depends on your attitude because what you believe will rule your life. A positive attitude will help you succeed in every situation. You are the only person on this planet who can make it better.

IT ONLY TAKES EVERYTHING YOU'VE GOT!

MENTAL DESSERT

Your living is determined not so much by what life brings to you as by the attitude you bring to life; not so much by what happens to you, as by the way your mind looks at what happened.

John Homer Miller

MENTAL APPETIZER

Just make up your mind at the very outset that your work is going to stand for quality ... that you are going to stamp superior quality upon everything that goes out of your hands. That whatever you do shall bear the hallmark of excellence.

Orison Swett Marden

MY MOTHER GAVE ME A WOODEN BOX

Momma was always a hard worker. From the time I was a little boy my mother instilled in me that I could do anything if I worked hard and applied myself. When I was 11 years old, I started cutting grass to make some money.

When I was 13, my mother gave me a wooden box that would change my life forever. On the outside of the box were the words, "The Secret of Success." When you opened up the box, there was a bold four-letter word inscribed "WORK." Many people ask me if the wooden box really exists. Of course it does! Everything in this book is true. Just to prove my point, turn the page and see Momma, the wooden box, and me.

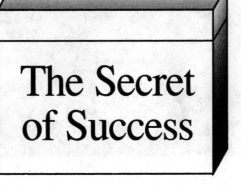

Not only do I still have the wooden box, entitled "The Secret of Success," but over the years I have found the "Ten Secrets of Success."

My desire to succeed and my experiences over the years have led me to these Ten Success Principles. No matter what you dream or attempt in this life, these principles are fundamental truths about success that need to be clearly understood.

Secret of Success #1
There are no secrets of success.

All of the truths, principles, and disciplines have been around since the beginning of mankind. There is nothing new under the heavens. Every day, we all get up under the same sky. The only difference is, we all see different horizons.

Secret of Success #2
Your life only becomes better when you become better.

If your career, marriage, job, and life are to improve, you must improve. You must change. In the mirror you are looking at the problem and the solution. It begins with you making a decision. The people who reach their potential no matter what their background or profession, think in terms of improvement.

Secret of Success # 3
You cannot have a positive life and a negative mind.

The Apostle Paul said, "Do not be conformed to this world, but be transformed by the renewing of your mind." Don't let the junk, doubt, and negativity of this world latch onto your mind, but every day, fill your mind with positive thoughts, productive information, and education. It takes strength of character to maintain a positive mind. Learn to discipline your mind. It is not the mountain you conquer, but your mind.

Secret of Success # 4
Success is for everyone.

Too many people misunderstand success. They think success is due to some genius, luck, or other thing which we do not possess. The reality is that success is knowing who you are, determining what your purpose in life is, and helping others along the way. This is the way we become fulfilled as human beings. Success is not about acquiring something. Success is about being fulfilled because you are growing to reach your full potential and you are helping others in the journey of life.

Secret of Success # 5
There can be no success without sacrifice.

Be willing to pay the price. Nothing of value in life comes easy. You must resolve to yourself to do whatever it takes to accomplish your desires and dreams. Whether it is working through tough times in your marriage or trying to lose weight, remember, no pain no gain. If you want to accomplish great things, be willing to sacrifice much. Success takes sacrifice. Success involves making choices and choice means sacrifice. The two go hand in hand.

Secret of Success # 6
Success is achieved in inches, not miles.

Most people never realize how close they are to attaining their dreams because they give up too soon. Little by little and inch by inch, it's a cinch. Everything in life takes dedication and time. The people who win in life are the people who harness the power of patience and persistence.

Secret of Success # 7
"Before anything else, getting ready is the secret of success." Henry Ford

You need to identify what you want to do, where you want to go, who you want to be, and what you want to accomplish. You do this by setting goals. Goals will help you determine priorities and help you constantly move toward your destination. Your goals will map out your actions, and your actions will create results.

Secret of Success #8
Your success is conceived in the mind, but your words give it life.

The tongue, through words, has the ability to build and to destroy. Words are not cheap. Words are the bridge into your future, because we believe everything that comes out of our own mouths. Make sure your words are always positive. They will create your world. Get so excited about planning your triumphs, you don't leave time to complain about your past losses.

Secret of Success #9
The greatest enemy of tomorrow's success is today's success.

A friend once told me, "The minute you think you have arrived is when you have departed." And he was right. Do not allow yourself to become complacent. Stay hungry. No matter what you've accomplished, or where you've been, there's always room for growth, improvement, and learning more. Don't let success go to your head, or settle into a comfort zone. Continue to move on to greater growth. Earl Wilson said, "If what you did yesterday still looks pretty good, then you haven't done enough today."

Secret of Success #10
None of the Secrets of Success will work unless you do!
Hard work is the mother of all success. Having goals is important. Passionate focus is vital. Knowledge is crucial. However, without work it is meaningless.

P.S. No amount of success at the office can compensate for failure at home.

IT ONLY TAKES EVERYTHING YOU'VE GOT!

MENTAL DESSERT

The quality of a person's life is in direct proportion to their commitment to excellence, regardless of the chosen field of endeavor.

Vincent T. Lombardi
(1913 - 1970)

MENTAL APPETIZER

*Success... seems to be
connected with action.
Successful men keep moving.
They make mistakes,
but they don't quit.*

Conrad Hilton

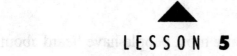

LESSON 5

I HAVE LOTS OF WEAKNESSES, BUT TAKING ACTION IS NOT ONE OF THEM

The German poet Johann Wolfgang von Goethe once said, "Thinking is easy, acting is difficult, and to put one's thoughts into action is the most difficult thing in the world." I believe he was right and that is why so few people follow through on their ideas or dreams.

Throughout high school, college, and my career, I have always been surrounded by people who were smarter, more talented, better educated, wealthier, or anything else you can add to the mix. The only thing that ever gave me an edge was that I always took Action!

If an idea came to me or a goal was set, I Just Did It. The best method for moving from idea or dream to action is summed up in these words of Nike's footwear commercial-- "Just Do It!"

The best way to make sure you are constantly moving and taking action is to set goals. Goals give you something concrete to focus on, and that has a positive impact on your Action.

Unfortunately, while most people have heard about goals, most do not have them.

ABOUT GOALS

Even though there are thousands of different definitions for goals, here is my K.I.S.S. version (keep it short and simple): A goal is a dream with a deadline.

Goals and goal-setting serve multiple purposes. They help you to determine priorities and stick with what is important. No one ever fulfills his purpose or develops his potential without goals.

Goals keep your attention on the present. Have you ever met someone who always talked about what she was going to be and as time passed, she did nothing? To be successful you must live and work in the present -- TODAY! Now is when you have the opportunity to actually accomplish something.

Goals help you keep score. Why do you think all sports have goals? Picture a basketball game without basketball goals. Picture a football game without goals. Picture a hockey or soccer game without goals. How could you keep score? How would you know who won the game? You wouldn't. Goals will let you know what kind of progress you are making or if you have gotten off track. They help you keep score. Your goals direct your actions, and your actions create results.

GOALS WORK

Growing up, I had a stuttering problem. I can remember the pain as a young child of hearing others ridiculing and making fun of the way I talked. I am not quite sure when it happened, but I made it my goal that I was not going to be made fun of any more. Over the years, I worked on my speech and by the time I graduated from college, it had improved tremendously. But that was not enough. I wanted to become not just a good oral communicator, but a great public speaker. So I wrote it down as a goal. Over the next couple of years, I took classes in Dale Carnegie, joined Toastmasters International, read an average of two books per month, and increased my vocabulary. Today, I am a member of the National Speakers Association and travel all over the country speaking to large organizations and get paid for it. I had a goal, and today I am living it. Writing down and pursuing my goal worked for me, has worked for others, and will work for you!

SOME PRACTICAL TIPS ON GOAL - SETTING

- Write them down. Once you write it down you are committed. The shortest pencil is better than a long memory.
- Be specific. Spell out what you intend to do.
- Make sure you have three to five specific goals in the following areas:

★**Personal Goals**: This area deals with the things intimate to you from saving money and buying a home to taking vacations and strengthening relationships.

★**Professional Goals**: This area deals with your job. From increasing your pay or starting a new business to closing a big sale or being promoted.

★**Self-Developmental Goals**: This area deals with having a game plan for your:
- Intellectual life (Reading books, listening to tapes, taking courses)
- Spiritual Life (Going to church, reading the bible, praying or giving to charity)
- Physical Life (Exercise program, balanced diet, and annual check'ups)

- Make sure they are achievable. Your goals need to be motivating, not intimidating.
- Make them measurable. That way you will know when you have accomplished them.
- Give them a deadline. Without some kind of deadline, most goals never become reality. They stay a wish or a dream. Always write a completion date for your goal.
- Adjust as necessary. Do not keep a goal you reach too easily or one you never reach. Things may change in your life, so learn to be flexible.
- Review your goals daily. Look at your goals daily. Keep the vision in front of you. Put them in your daily planner or checkbook. Tape them to your bathroom mirror or closet door.

Goal-setting takes time, discipline, courage, and patience. There are plenty of distractions and temptations along the way. But when you make the commitment, be prepared for great things to happen. Sometimes you have to do something you have never done to accomplish something you have always wanted. To Take Action, you have to begin somewhere, and setting goals is the best place to start.

IT ONLY TAKES EVERYTHING YOU'VE GOT!

MENTAL DESSERT

" There is nothing brilliant
nor outstanding in my record,
except perhaps this one thing:
I do the things that I believe
ought to be done..... And
when I make up my mind
to do a thing, I act."

Theodore Roosevelt
(1858 - 1919)

MENTAL APPETIZER

The ability to have or to find information when you need it and then take action is what gets things done in life.

Julio Melara

LESSON 6

WORDS ARE NOT CHEAP!

It has been said that we will live one-fifth of our lives speaking. Yet I am amazed every day at the number of people who waste and spend their words so cheaply.

One of the most powerful truths you can ever understand is that the tongue has the ability to build up or destroy. I have seen this truth affect people both positively and negatively. I'm like Abraham Lincoln, who said, "Everything I am and everything I hope to be, I owe to my mother." As I was growing up, my mother told me over and over again that I was smart and handsome and that I could do anything I set my mind to. Those words still ring in my ears today.

On the other hand, I have a friend who grew up in a family where his mother didn't say much and his father constantly called him a bum or idiot. Unfortunately, those words became reality, and after a while he got hooked on drugs. I don't know what else could have led him to this, but I do know that he went through a lot of pain simply because his parents did not account for their words.

WORDS HAVE POWER

Words have power because they create your world. It is important to watch what you say about yourselves because this affects your self-confidence, self-concept and self-esteem. Why? More than anything that anyone else says, you believe what comes out of your own mouth. That is what it means when people say life is a self-fulfilling prophecy. Refuse to release words of defeat, depression, and discouragement. Your words are life, and you must bring your tongue under control. Talk health, happiness, and prosperity to every person you meet. Make your family and friends feel that there is something worthwhile in them. By thinking and speaking positively, you open up the doors to make your optimism come true.

I am not suggesting that you deny the reality of an adverse situation or a major problem you are facing, but that you be solution-oriented and on the lookout for the sunny side of everything. The great Abraham Lincoln summed it up best when he said, "An optimist is one who sees an opportunity in every difficulty. A pessimist is one who sees a difficulty in every opportunity." He spoke the truth!

THINK BEFORE YOU SPEAK

If you don't think before you speak it is like shooting without aiming. I say the word "think" because most do not, and because you can use it as an acronym to make sure your words are productive powerful, and:

Truthful- If you always tell the truth you will never have to remember what you said.

Helpful- To the proportion that you help other people either by teaching, training, coaching, or correcting, they will help you.

Informative- The value of the knowledge you share or education you give is determined by its ability to help others grow.

Necessary- Silence cannot by misquoted. Never discuss your problems with someone who can't solve them. Know when to talk and when to listen.

Kind-   Life is too short. Be silent instead of discussing the shortcomings or weak nesses of others. If what you say to someone can't be said to everyone, then say it to no one.

LEARN MORE WORDS

Not only is it important to choose your words carefully, but you must have an array of words to choose from in your vocabulary. The English language has more than 450,000 words. Most of our daily conversations are made up of a mere 400 words. That means we only use .0008 percent of words available to us, and unfortunately, some of the most common used are I, me, and my.

While going to college full time and working at a business newspaper full time, I began to realize how limited my vocabulary was. Then I started reading and listening to material that reinforced the fact that there is a direct correlation between the number of words you use in your vocabulary and the amount of money you will make in your career. Research by management and human resources experts have confirmed that no matter what the field of employment, people with large vocabularies (those able to speak clearly, using simple and descriptive words) are the most likely to accomplish their goals.

That is why in my junior year in college, I committed to learning one new word a day, its definition and its pronunciation. After college I purchased a copy of Dr. Denis Waitley's *500 MasterWord Series* and began to dedicate myself to learning more words.

This is a powerful exercise. Your ability to articulate and orally communicate will determine how far you can go. The more you learn, the more you earn. Well-chosen and carefully selected words can close the sale, enhance relationships, negotiate your raise and help you attain your goals. You only have one chance to make a first impression.

Your ability to communicate with other people is a vital measure for success. While knowledge and information are the most powerful forces for achievement, language skill is the key that unlocks the door. Commit to learning more words and becoming an effective communicator.

IT ONLY TAKES EVERYTHING YOU'VE GOT!

MENTAL DESSERT

If you wait until the wind and the weather are just right, you will never plant anything and never harvest anything.

Ecclesiastes 11:4

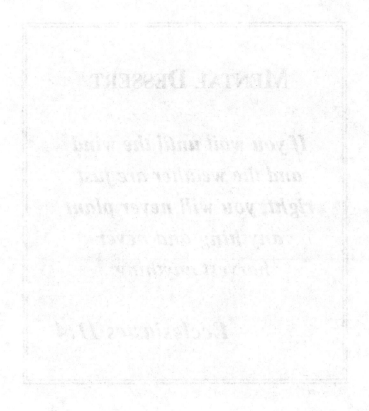

MENTAL APPETIZER

I would never have amounted to anything were it not for adversity. I was forced to come up the hard way.

J. C. Penney

LESSON 7

THE VALUE OF FAILING

One of my all-time favorite commercials on television features Michael Jordan walking into the basketball arena. The fans are going crazy and they are chanting "Michael, Michael, Michael." As he is walking and hearing his name chanted over and over again, he is having a conversation with himself inside his head. He says to himself, "I've missed over 9,000 shots in my career, lost over 300 games, 26 times I took the game-winning shot and missed. Because of these failures, I'm a success!" What a powerful message!

As I have talked to people about success, I have found that their greatest fear is failure. After talking with many successful people at the top of their field, it became evident that they all had the ability to fail. All of them have had setbacks, made mistakes and have fallen down many times. We all fail from time to time. It's whether you're going to fail and learn from the experience or allow failure to discourage you and move you backward that counts. Most people do not understand or handle failure very well, but it is an inevitable part of life. If you want to continue to grow and progress on the success journey, you need to learn from failure.

"The difference between greatness and mediocrity is often how an individual views mistakes," said Nelson Boswell. He was right. Unsuccessful people spend a good portion of their lives avoiding risks or making decisions because they fear failure. They do not understand that success is based on their ability to fail and then get up and keep going. Successful people do not allow failure to go to their heads. They understand that often times the biggest lessons they learn have been when they have had setbacks, made mistakes or gone through adversity. Why? Because it is when you fail that you stop and take time to reflect, contemplate, and analyze how you can change your current situations.

As I write this chapter, I am remembering all the jobs and times I have failed in my life. Here is a list of jobs you will not find on my resume' but lessons that have lasted a lifetime:

- Started cutting grass for profit at age 11
  Lesson learned: It is important to give things a clean, professional look.

- Stock clerk at a local food store
  Lesson learned: Making sure that if I am going to sell something, the merchandise needs to be in stock.

- Porter at a used car lot
  Lesson learned: Serving is the gateway to selling. And if I made the car sparkle, people were more attracted to it.

- Dishwasher at local restaurant
  Lesson learned: Somebody always has to do the job no one else wants to do. Also, most people leave a lot of food on their plates. (They do not finish what they start.)

- A janitor at an office building
  Lesson learned: The importance of cleanliness as it relates to image.

- Fry and prep cook at a steak house
  Lesson learned: The importance of preparation and the impact of the right presentation.

- Merchandiser for Gallo Wine
  Lesson learned: How to arrange and position things so that people will have a greater desire to buy.

- Construction helping hand (lug wood and supplies from one place to another)
  Lesson learned: I do not want to do this for the rest of my life.

- Sold newspaper subscription for daily paper
  Lesson learned: The joy of rejection-- had to knock on at least 30 doors before I ever sold one subscription.

- Shipping clerk at a plumbing supply house
  Lesson learned: Delivering your product or service on time is just as important as selling it.

- Breakfast cook at a 24 hour restaurant stop
  Lesson learned: How to do 15 things at once. Also, learned about the weird things people like to eat on their eggs.

- Cleaned cars at detailing shop
  Lesson learned: The importance of details. (Washing vs. Detailing) You can pay $15 just to wash the outside of the car or $150 to clean the car inside and out and cover all the details. Details are a pain, but details are valuable.

- Shoe salesman at a retail store
  Lesson learned: To sell customers what they want and like. Also, learned to compliment people and be sincere.

- Busboy at a local diner
  Lesson learned: People enjoy being served with a smile and they love a clean table.

- Courier for business newspaper
  Lesson learned: Even though it was one of the lowest jobs in the company, the organization could not function without the deliveries made. The messenger is just as important as the message.

In every one of these jobs, I can remember experiencing some type of failure and frustration. But it never stopped me from trying to do my best. The biggest lessons I learned came from setbacks. They gave me determination! I learned quickly what Zig Ziglar says, "Failure is an event, not a person."

My friend Jeffrey Gitomer says there are only five degrees of failing and areas we all constantly need to check:

1. Failing to do your best.
2. Failing to learn.
3. Failing to accept responsibility.
4. Failing to meet quotas or goals.
5. Failing to have a positive attitude.

Every one of these areas you control. The last one is the most critical because, when you have the right attitude, failure is neither fatal nor final.

Leadership expert Warren Bennis interviewed 70 of the nation's top performers in various fields and found that none of them viewed their mistakes as failures. When talking about them, they referred to them as "learning experiences," "tuition paid," "detours," and "opportunities for growth."[1]

Successful people don't do well on the negative consequences of failure; they focus on learning from their mistakes and thinking how they can improve their situations and themselves. Do you recognize any of the following failures?:

Sir Winston Churchill (1874 -1965), British Statesman
Churchill's father considered his son so "dull" that he doubted whether he could ever earn a living. Churchill failed the entrance exams to Sandhurst twice and was taken out of Harrow so that he could study with a "crammer" (tutor).

Giacomo Puccini (1858 -1924), Italian Opera Composer
Puccini's first music teacher gave up on teaching him music because he had "no talent."

Albert Einstein (1879 -1955), German Physicist
Einstein spoke haltingly until he was nine and after that responded to questions only after much

deliberation. His poor performance in all classes except math prompted a teacher to ask him to drop out of school, telling Einstein he'd never amount to anything. Einstein failed his first entrance exam at Zurich's Polytechnic Institute.

Sir Isaac Newton (1642-1727), English Scientist
Newton was allowed to get an education only because he proved to be a complete failure in running his family's farm. He started out in the lowest form of his school.

Pablo Picasso (1881-1973), Spanish Painter
Picasso could barely read or write at age 10 and he was considered a "hopeless pupil" because he refused to learn mathematics.

Thomas Edison (1847-1931), U.S. Inventor
Edison's teachers described him as "addled," his father thought he was a "dunce", and his head-masters warned that Edison "would never make a success of anything."

Bill Gates (1955-   ), Dropped out of college to start his own business.

Someone's opinion of you does not have to be your reality. You create your own world when you transform your mind.

CHANGE YOUR THINKING

Most of you have heard this perspective on failure, yet few have tried this approach. The great hotel executive Conrad Hilton said, "Successful people keep moving. They make mistakes, but they do not quit." Only people who attempt nothing never fail. People who accomplish things face setbacks repeatedly. Here are five principles I have learned over the years that have helped me and will help you handle failure:

1. Don't Take Failing Personally

As I grow older, I have realized that when I was younger I took failure a lot more personally. All of my mistakes looked a lot bigger. Over the years, I have realized and learned that everything I do is not going to be successful. I do not beat up on myself anymore. Instead I tell myself "I'll do better next time" or " I now know what to do or not to do." Making mistakes is like eating: it is something you will keep doing as long as you are alive. The bottom line-- learn from the experience, learn to live with it, and move on.

2. Make Failing a Learning Experience

Your willingness to learn from failure and the ability to overcome that obstacle are key components to your success in life. To be successful, you need to develop the ability to learn from your mistakes. I do not know who said "Failure isn't failure unless you don't learn from it," but they were right! The tests of life are not to break you, but to make you!

3. Do Not Let Failing Keep You Down

I always tell people you do not drown because you fall in the water. You drown because you stay there. Everyone gets knocked down in life, but it is your ability to keep getting up that determines your success. When you do fail, learn what you can from your mistake or the experience and then get back on your feet and keep marching forward. The great Henry Ford summarized this feeling best when he said, "Failure is the opportunity to begin again more intelligently."

4. Keep Your Sense of Humor

I know this may not be scientific, but I have learned to laugh at myself and the world. It is easy to laugh when you are having a good time and things are going great. However, it is important to laugh when things are going wrong. Laughing relieves stress and helps you put your mistake into perspective. As you go through your life and make mistakes or fall down, keep everything in a positive and humorous perspective. Many times when I am speaking at conferences or conventions and I hear my two- minute introduction of who I am and what some of my accomplishments are, I laugh inside my head because I know if they read off a list of all the times I failed, we would be there all day.

5. Do Not Give In or Give Up

I mentioned earlier that there is a price for success. Failure comes easily to everyone, but the price for success is perseverance. B.C. Forbes said, "History has demonstrated that the most notable winners usually encountered heartbreaking obstacles before they triumphed. They finally won because they refused to become discouraged by their defeats." There are thousands of examples in the worlds of business, politics, athletics, education, and other areas, but here is my all-time favorite:

If you sometimes get discouraged, consider this fellow:
He dropped out of grade school.
Ran a business.
Went broke.
Took 15 years to pay off his bills.
Took a wife.
She died.
Ran for the House of Representatives.
Lost twice.
Ran for the Senate.
Lost twice.

Delivered a speech that became a classic.
Audience indifferent.
Attacked daily by the press and despised by half
the country.

Despite all this, imagine how many people all over
the world have been inspired by this awkward,
rumpled, brooding man who signed his name simply,
A. Lincoln.

Failure can make all of us better or bitter. Let's
follow Abe's example.

IT ONLY TAKES EVERYTHING YOU'VE GOT!

MENTAL DESSERT

*Failure is Success
if We Learn From it.*

Malcolm Forbes

MENTAL APPETIZER

*The Time
is Always Right
to do What is Right.*

Author Unknown

LESSON 8

TRUTH IS HEAVY:
THAT'S WHY SO FEW PEOPLE CARRY IT

One of my first mentors used to tell me, "Always tell the truth and then you do not ever have to remember what you said." My mother constantly reminded me to work hard and always tell the truth. She told me that if I followed those two guidelines, I would always have a good name. One of the Proverbs in the Scriptures says, "A good name is more desirable than great riches."

All of these statements are true but in very short supply these days. Sadly, integrity is a vanishing commodity today. The dictionary defines integrity in terms of soundness of moral character and adherence to ethical principles. It is a standard of personal morals and ethics. Here is an important truth about integrity: You must realize that there are no degrees of integrity. Either you have it or you do not. But probably the best definition I have ever heard was that integrity is not what you do, as much as who you are. Integrity is not just knowing what is right, but doing it!

Why all this talk about truth and integrity? A commitment to a life of integrity in every situation demonstrates that your word is your bond. You do what is right, not what is fashionable. You know that truth is absolute, not a device with which to manipulate others or situations. You are who you are, no matter where you are and who you are with. Programming this into your conscience will put you so far ahead of the rest in the long run that you will wonder why everyone does not do the same.

I can remember one holiday season walking in to Sears to purchase an electrical drill and some tools. Two young college students were working the cash register when I got into the long and crowded line. It was obvious that both guys were overwhelmed with the Christmas rush. By the time I got to the cash register there was commotion all over the place and the students started rushing and just putting things into bags. It was amazing how quickly one of them rang up my purchase, but I was glad to be out of the line. As I was heading out the door, I checked to make sure the drills, tools, and receipts were all there. They were. The problem was that I had not been charged for the drill. The line was long and I thought for a split second that it was the cashier's mistake and not my fault. However, I wanted to sleep in peace that night so I went back to let the clerk know he needed to charge me for the electric drill. He looked at me with a glazed look and said, "Who are you, Honest Joe?"

It was obvious he knew what he had done but did not care. Not only did I pay for the drill, but that night I slept fantastic. I had done the right thing.

DOING THE RIGHT THING

Integrity means always doing what is right. Synonyms for integrity include honesty, trust-worthiness, and honor. Implanting this in your consciousness will not only make you feel good, but make you a winner in the long run when the stakes are the highest. Why? First, because one of the laws that God has in place is the law of sowing and reaping. You see, if you think the IRS will not catch you or that cheating on your spouse occasionally will not hurt, you need to remember that sooner or later you will have to pay. A person with integrity does not have divided loyalties. He is single-minded and has nothing to hide or fear. Secondly, when your values and actions do not match, you have become a hypocrite. Hypocrites do not have credibility, therefore it paralyzes their ability to succeed. Why throw your reputation away, live with guilt, or bring shame to your family? You only build credibility by telling the truth. You cannot lead people or run a successful company unless people believe you. The bottom line is that lying and dishonesty are bad business.

Integrity affects all aspects of your lives. Can you think of any successful relationship without integrity? I doubt it. All are based on mutual trust. Break trust and you break the relationship. We all struggle daily with situations that demand decisions between what we want to do and what we ought to do. Integrity establishes the ground rules for resolving these tensions. It will not allow your mouth to violate your heart. When integrity is the referee, you will be consistent; your beliefs will be mirrored by your conduct. There will not be a difference between what you appear to be and what your family knows you are.

Here are a few truths regarding integrity that will help you live the high life:

1) Always give others credit that is rightfully theirs.

2) Always be honest and open about who you really are.

3) Always set high standards of ethics for yourself.

4) Always defend your convictions and beliefs, despite social pressures or political correctness.

5) Always give your best, even in the worst of times.

6) Always tell the truth, even if it hurts.

Socrates said, "The first key to greatness is to be in reality what we appear to be." To earn trust from your family, employees, and friends, you must be authentic. For that to happen, your words and lives must match. Remember how people called President Lincoln "Honest Abe". What do they call you?

The great Dwight Eisenhower said, "In order to be a leader, a man must have their confidence. Hence, the supreme quality for a leader is unquestionably integrity. Without it, no real success is possible. No matter whether it is on a section gang, a football field, in an army, or in an office. If a man's associates find him guilty of being phony, if they find that he lacks forthright integrity, he will fail. His teachings and actions must square with each other. The first great need, therefore, is integrity and high purpose."

Remember, integrity is 24 hours a day, seven days a week. Personal integrity knows no season and does not change with the wind or hinge on the stock market report. You either have it or you do not. Commit TODAY to live a life of truth and integrity.

IT ONLY TAKES EVERYTHING YOU'VE GOT!

MENTAL DESSERT

*When wealth is lost,
nothing is lost; when
health is lost, something
is lost; when character
is lost, all is lost.*

Billy Graham

MENTAL APPETIZER

"Desire isn't worth anything without discipline"

Julio Melara

LESSON 9

SELF-DISCIPLINE IS A LEARNED ART

In reading about the lives of great people, I found that self-discipline came first with all of them. What is self-discipline? The dictionary defines it as bringing oneself under control. The word self-control comes from the Greek root word meaning "to grip" or "take hold of." This word describes people who are willing to take hold of their lives and take control of areas that will bring them success or failure. To achieve and accomplish your dreams you must take responsibility for your own self-discipline and personal growth. The word discipline originated from two Latin words: Discipulus, which means "pupil", and descire, which means "to learn." Putting both of them together means "to teach." Translated another way, self-discipline is your willingness and ability to teach yourself about the total essence of your being.

All of the other "lessons" in this book are absolutely worthless without self-discipline. The death of your dreams or anything else you want to accomplish is certain without self-discipline. The reason most people never accomplish the things they want to is because of issues going on inside of them rather than outside of them.

Some people think self-discipline is doing without. It's not! Self-discipline is doing within. It is a mental exercise-- the memorization of thoughts and emotions that will override the current information stored in your subconscious. Through constant repetition of these new thoughts in your mind, along with concentrated self-talk, you will be able to create your new self image. You will begin to see yourself as a stronger person. You will gain self-respect and this will fuel your self-confidence. Psychologist Abraham Heschel said it best, "Self-respect is the fruit of discipline."

IT'S NOT EASY

Of course, self-discipline is not easy. Initially, discipline comes from others. Your parents or teachers told you what to do and when to do it, and you did it. The key is to shift that externally focused discipline and make it part of your daily routine. This is accomplished by answering two questions: First, what do I want to accomplish? Second, what do I need to do to get there?

In other words, you are on the road to self-discipline when you do what you need to do rather that what you want to do. The true mark of maturity comes when what you want and what you need are the same.

START SMALL AND START TODAY

What you are going to be tomorrow, you are becoming today. How disciplined are you? Take this quick test and look in the mirror. (Be honest with yourself.) Check off the appropriate column for each listing on the next page.

How Disciplined Are You ?

1. Words
   a. Do you talk too much?
   b. Do you talk too little?
   c. Do you talk too loudly or too softly?
   d. Do you talk too quickly or too slowly?
   e. Do you speak harshly or sharply?
   f. Do you discipline yourself not to gossip?

2. Thoughts
   a. Are you disciplined with your thoughts, or do you let them run rampant?
   b. Are you a good listener?

3. Appetite
   a. Do you eat too much or too little?
   b. Do you eat too fast?
   c. Do you eat a well-balanced diet?
   d. Do you drink plenty of water?

4. Exercise/Rest/Entertainment
   a. Do you get proper exercise?
   b. Do you allow time for rest and relaxation?
   c. Do you sleep too much or too little?
   d. Do you get the right balance of fun, leisure, and entertainment?

A	B	C
Not Disciplined	A Little Disciplined	Very Disciplined
❏	❏	❏
❏	❏	❏
❏	❏	❏
❏	❏	❏
❏	❏	❏
❏	❏	❏
❏	❏	❏
❏	❏	❏
❏	❏	❏
❏	❏	❏
❏	❏	❏
❏	❏	❏
❏	❏	❏
❏	❏	❏
❏	❏	❏
❏	❏	❏

5. Housework/Car/Cleanup
   a. Are you disciplined in keeping your house in good order?
   b. Are you disciplined in taking care of your car?
   c. Are you disciplined in cleaning up after yourself?

6. Personal Grooming
   a. Hair
   b. Clothing
   c. Nails

7. Money
   a. Do you spend too much or too little?
   b. Do you discipline yourself to give to church or charities?

8. Family/Helping Others
   a. Do you spend quality time with your family?
   b. Are you disciplined about disciplining your children?
   c. How disciplined are you in helping other people?

9. Promptness/Integrity/Honesty
   a. How disciplined are you about being prompt and on time?
   b. How disciplined are you with keeping your word?

A Not Disciplined	**B** A Little Disciplined	**C** Very Disciplined
❏	❏	❏
❏	❏	❏
❏	❏	❏
❏	❏	❏
❏	❏	❏
❏	❏	❏
❏	❏	❏
❏	❏	❏
❏	❏	❏
❏	❏	❏
❏	❏	❏
❏	❏	❏

c. Does your split-second timing keep you living on the edge, or do you plan ahead?

d. Do you discipline yourself to keep the law? (i.e., speed limit, no parking sign, etc.)

10. Consideration of Others
a. Do you discipline yourself to be considerate of other people's time frames?
b. Do you discipline yourself to abide within the framework of given guidelines?

Scoring: Give yourself:
1 point for each checkmark in Column A
2 points for each checkmark in Column B
3 points for each checkmark in Column C

Now add up each column.
Then add the column totals together.
If your score is 0 - 33, you're not disciplined.
If your score is 34 - 66, you're somewhat disciplined.
If your score is 67 - 99, you're very disciplined.

	A Not Disciplined	B A Little Disciplined	C Very Disciplined
TOTAL	_____	_____	_____

Grand Total:_____

A	B	C
Not Disciplined	**A Little** Disciplined	**Very** Disciplined
❏	❏	❏
❏	❏	❏
❏	❏	❏
❏	❏	❏

If your score was low, the good news is that you can start developing self-discipline in a small way today. Below is an action plan that will help you begin. If you scored high, the good news is that you are on your way to success. However, be aware that success is far more difficult to live with than failure. You must constantly work on developing and perfecting your self-discipline just as an artist perfects a great piece of art.

SELF-DISCIPLINE IS ACTION!

As I was writing this book, many people asked me how I found time to get it done. How do I have time to keep my marriage going, run two companies, co-own another, work out two times per week, play tennis once a week, read the Bible and pray constantly, sit on a bank board, travel and give speeches, read three books a month, sleep, and still have time to write a book? My answer, "Self-Discipline." It was not fun getting up at 5 o'clock in the morning or being locked inside a room on Sundays to write when everyone else was enjoying their weekend. But the sacrifice was worth it! Writing this book was my goal. I knew what I needed to do and I did it. It is true-- when you do things you ought to do when you ought to do them, the day will come when you will do the things you want to do when you want to do them. Here are some small action plans that will make a big difference in your journey toward becoming disciplined:

- List three areas in your life that lack discipline.
- Prioritize the list in the order you want to conquer them.
- Look for some books and tapes that will give you information, instruction, and motivation to conquer each area.
- Find someone you respect (a person who has the trait you want) to hold you accountable.
- Spend 15 to 30 minutes each morning planning and getting focused in order to get control of the weak areas in your life.

- Spend at least 90 days working on one area before you go to the next. (It takes time--stay focused and be patient.)
- Reward yourself as you gain discipline in that area and celebrate with the person who holds you accountable.

Remember, having it all does not mean having it all at once. Start little by little and concentrate on one day at a time. It is the slow accumulation of discipline that will make a big difference throughout your life.

ONE FINAL WORD ON SELF-DISCIPLINE

In the final analysis, it is not doing the things we like to do, but doing the things we have to do that causes growth and makes us successful. Successful people are willing to do things unsuc-cessful people will not do. It is only when you have decided in your own mind to systematically plan, pursue, and carry out your goals that you have become self-disciplined and are on the road to success.

IT ONLY TAKES EVERYTHING YOU'VE GOT!

MENTAL DESSERT

*"One is not born into
the world to do
everything, but to
do something."*

*Henry David Thoreau
(1817 - 1862)*

MENTAL APPETIZER

"God doesn't require us to succeed; He only requires that you try."

Mother Teresa

THERE ARE NO DAYS OFF IN LIFE

I was having lunch one day with Dale Brown, former Louisiana State University head basketball coach, when he turned to me and said, "Julio, it's how you live between the beginning and end of the line that counts." I said, "Huh?" He asked, "When were you born?" "1964", I answered. Then he took a piece of paper and wrote:

Julio Melara

1964 —

He said it again, "The only thing that matters is how you live your life between the beginning and end of the line." I finally got it.

It does not matter when you were born, where you started, or where you are. What matters is this: What are you doing right now? Where are you headed? How are you going to get there? How will you finish?

Too many people simply let life happen to them. Only a very few decide what is going to happen to them. To just stay alive is not enough! Throughout this book I have shared some practical lessons on how to do more with your life than simply let it happen. It is not easy, but it is essential.

FINISH WHAT YOU START

In the end, your success is measured by your ability to complete things. You will only be able to accomplish things through persistence and perseverance. Calvin Coolidge put it this way: "Your ability to face setbacks and disappointment without giving up will be the measure of your ability to succeed." Most success gurus and philosophers agree you can never simply fail. However, you can give up trying. You need persistence and perseverance to achieve your goals and live your dreams.

Stop for a moment and think about the times you have fallen down in life. What did you learn from each struggle? What lesson did you learn from that adversity? Did you give up too soon? Did you look for the easy way out? Maybe there is an area in your life right now where you need to persevere. Make a commitment to fight through the storm.

You will need faith to persevere. Read the Bible or the writings of Thomas Edison, Dr. Norman Vincent Peale, William James and others. In every situation and circumstance since the beginning of mankind and throughout history, succeeding in life has meant persevering. Success demands perseverance. Hang on and you will succeed.

DON'T LISTEN TO THE WORLD

How do you begin to shift your paradigm? By realizing there are two worlds. There is the world, and there is your world. The world is society and all of the junk and cynicism promoted daily through the so called "news" and advertisements. It used to be that Walter Cronkite would end his newscast by saying, "And that's the way it is." Everyone trusted he was right. Today things have changed drastically. Shock value seems to have the highest premium in determining the value of a news story. The "ABC Evening News" and "60 Minutes" now compete with "Inside Edition" and "A Current Affair" for ratings. What's wrong with this picture? Are you spending more time watching television, or reading books? How much time do you spend listening to educational and motivational tapes instead of the radio?

Your mind is yours to fill with whatever you want. But observe closely what I am sharing with you. Society entices people to lay back and seek comfort. Look at all the advertisements today. They are designed to make you feel more comfortable and less challenged. Don't be fooled. You create your own world!

It is only by taking risks and being challenged that you will grow. Only by getting out of your comfort zone and being challenged will your skills be tested. It is only by working hard and being challenged that you will be transformed and experience the personal growth you want. Life is about growing, learning, and transforming your life daily. There is no such thing as a stable life. Everyday you are either growing or receding, increasing or decreasing, whether it's physically, spiritually, financially, or professionally.

It is up to you to constantly look for challenges to continue to grow and enjoy the success journey. Colin Wilson said, "When a butterfly has emerged, it can never turn back into a caterpillar." You will never be the same again when you take control of your mind.

THE CHOICE IS YOURS

The danger with any book is that a person who reads it will turn the last page and never think about it again. Don't let that be the case with you.

Nothing in life worth having comes easy. But through perseverance, continuing to grow, and working hard on yourself, a time will come when others will suddenly consider you an overnight success. It seems as though few ever see the adversity, pain, or perseverance successful people overcome in their journey. Most only notice the final outcome. It doesn't really matter because God knows and you know. When they ask you how you did it? You can tell them, "I realized there are no days off in life! I took responsibility for my life, maintained a positive attitude, worked hard, had discipline, and applied myself everyday. And when they ask you "what does it take to be successful?", you can tell them:

IT ONLY TAKES EVERYTHING YOU'VE GOT!